Theory of Music Exams

GRADE 5

2006

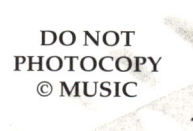

The Associated Board of the Royal Schools of Music

ABRSM Publishing

Also available Model Answers

Theory Paper Grade 5   2006   A

Duration 2 hours

This paper contains SEVEN questions, ALL of which should be answered.
Write your answers on this paper — no others will be accepted.
Answers must be written clearly and neatly — otherwise marks may be lost.

DO NOT PHOTOCOPY © MUSIC

TOTAL MARKS 100

1 (a) The following extract, which begins on the first beat of the bar, requires a different time signature for each bar. Put in the three correct time signatures.

Tarik O'Regan, *Care charminge Sleepe*

© Oxford University Press 2003
Extract reproduced by permission.

(6)

(b) (i) Describe the chords marked A, B and C in the extract below as I, II, IV or V. Also indicate whether the lowest note of the chord is the root (a), 3rd (b) or 5th (c). The key is E♭ major.

Vanhal, Sonatina No. 3

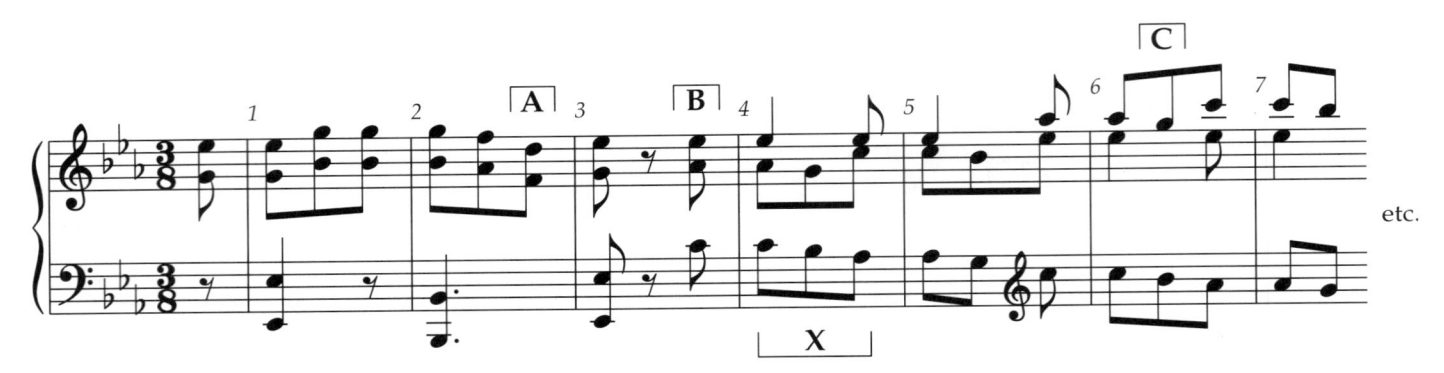

Chord A ....

Chord B ....

Chord C ....

(6)

(ii) Rewrite the left-hand part of bar 4 (marked X) so that it sounds the same, but using the alto C clef. Remember to put in the key signature.

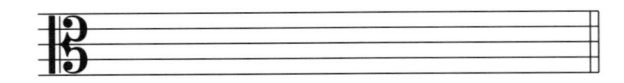

(3)

2 Describe fully each of the numbered melodic intervals (e.g. major 2nd). [10]

J. S. Bach, Flute Sonata in G, BWV 1039

Intervals:

1 ....

2 ....

3 ....

4 ....

5 ....

3 The following melody is written for clarinet in B♭. Transpose it *down* a major 2nd, as it will sound at concert pitch. Do *not* use a key signature but remember to put in all necessary sharp, flat or natural signs. [10]

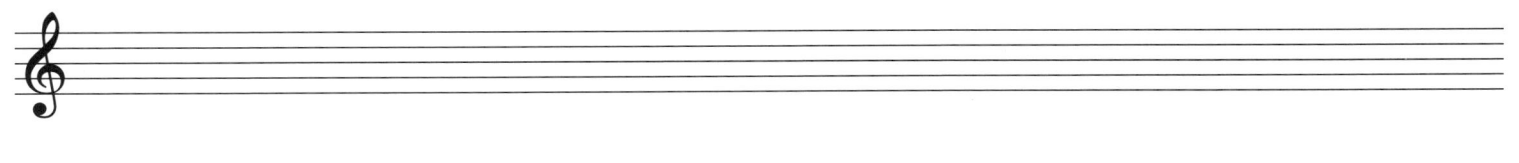

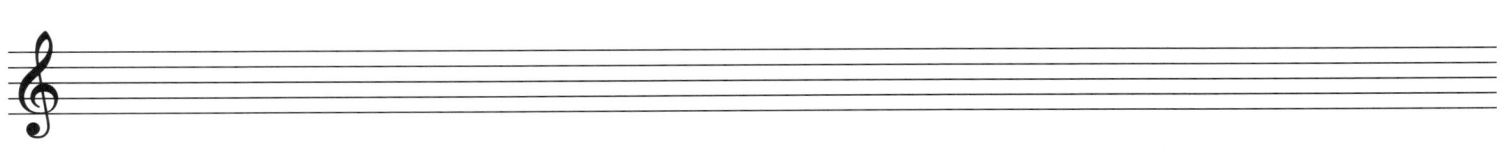

Shostakovich, Symphony No. 8

Extract from Symphony No. 8
© Copyright 1943 by Boosey & Hawkes Music Publishers Ltd
for the UK, British Commonwealth (excl. Canada) and Eire
Reproduced by permission.

4 The following extract is from a piano piece, *Italian Fishermen's Song*, by Schumann. Look at it and then answer the questions that follow.

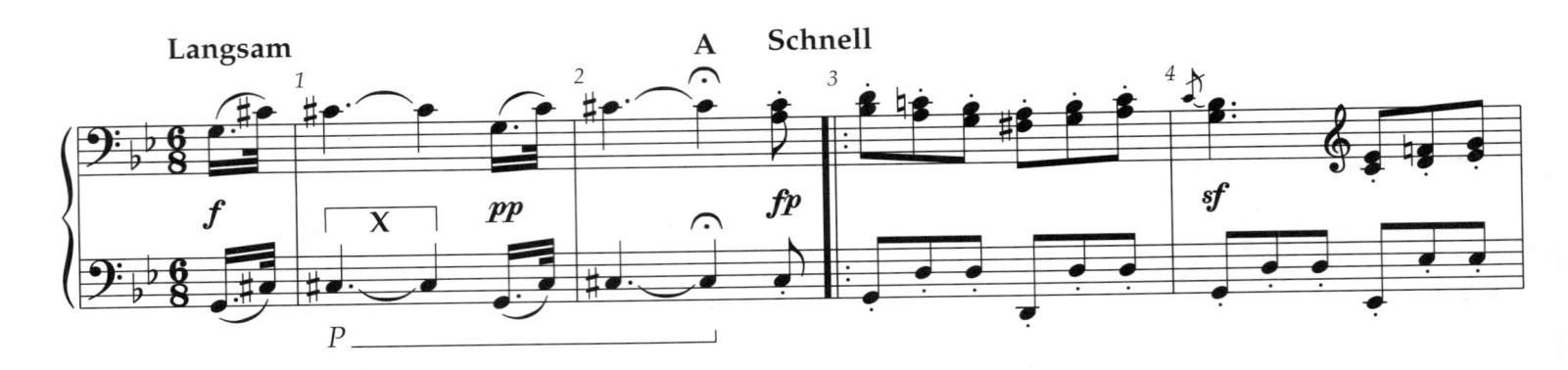

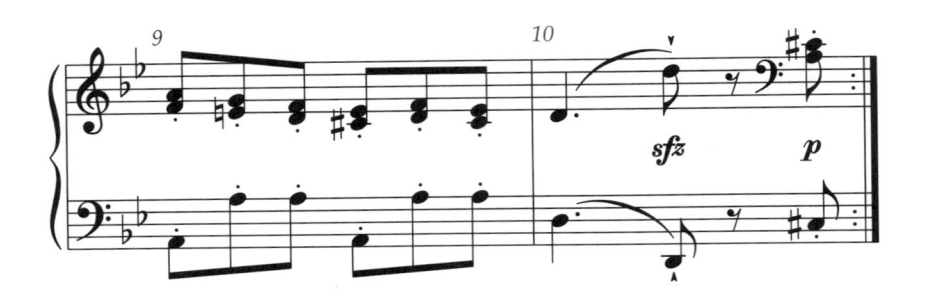

(a) Give the meaning of:

Langsam .... (2)

P⌐⎯⎯⌐ (bars 1–2) .... (2)

Schnell (bars 2–3) .... (2)

sfz (bar 10) .... (2)

:‖ (bar 10) .... (2)

(b) (i) **Mark clearly on the music**, using the appropriate capital letter for identification, one example of each of the following. Also give the bar number of each of your answers, as shown in the answer to **A**.

A   a pause. Bar .....2.....

B   an acciaccatura (circle the note concerned). Bar ....

C   the melodic interval of an augmented 4th. Bar ....   (4)

(ii) Complete the following statements:

The tied notes in the left-hand part of bar 1 (marked X) are worth .... (2)
semiquavers (sixteenth-notes) in total.

At the beginning of bar 4, the music is in the key of ....

but at the beginning of bar 6 it reaches the key of ....   (4)

(c) (i) Rewrite the first right-hand chord of bar 3 so that it sounds the same, but using the tenor C clef. Remember to put in the clef and the key signature.

(4)

(ii) Underline *one* of the following instruments that could play the left-hand part of bars 1–2 so that it sounds at the same pitch.

       trombone   oboe   viola   clarinet   (2)

(iii) Now name the family of standard orchestral instruments to which the instrument you have underlined belongs and state its highest-sounding member.

Family .... Instrument .... (4)

5 (a) Using semibreves (whole-notes), write one octave **ascending** of the **melodic** minor scale that has this key signature. Begin on the tonic and remember to include any additional sharp, flat or natural signs.

(b) Using semibreves (whole-notes), write one octave **descending** of the major scale that begins on the given note. Do *not* use a key signature but put in all necessary sharp or flat signs.

6 EITHER

(a) Compose a complete melody for unaccompanied violin or oboe, using the given opening. Indicate the tempo and other performance directions, including any that might be particularly required for the instrument chosen. The complete melody should be eight bars long.

Instrument for which the melody is written: ....

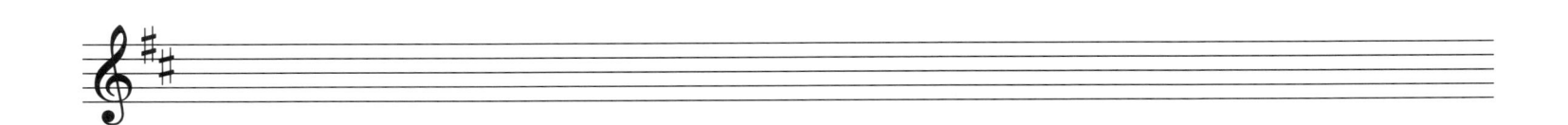

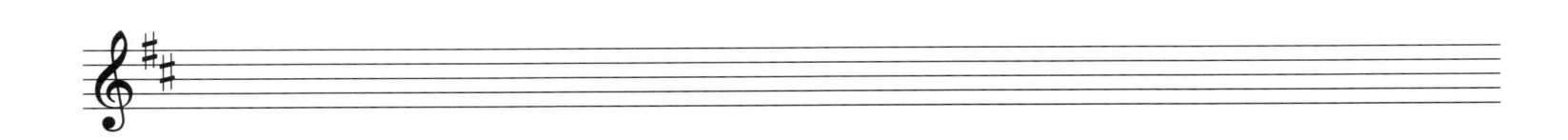

OR

(b) Compose a complete melody to the following words for a solo voice. Write each syllable under the note or notes to which it is to be sung. Also indicate the tempo and other performance directions as appropriate.

> The river glares in the sun
> Like a torrent of molten glass.
>
> *Rudyard Kipling*

7 Suggest suitable progressions for two cadences in the following melody by indicating ONLY ONE chord (I, II, IV or V) at each of the places marked A – E. You do not have to indicate the position of the chords, or to state which note is in the bass.

Show the chords:

EITHER (a) by writing I, II etc. or any other recognized symbols on the dotted lines below;

OR (b) by writing notes on the staves.

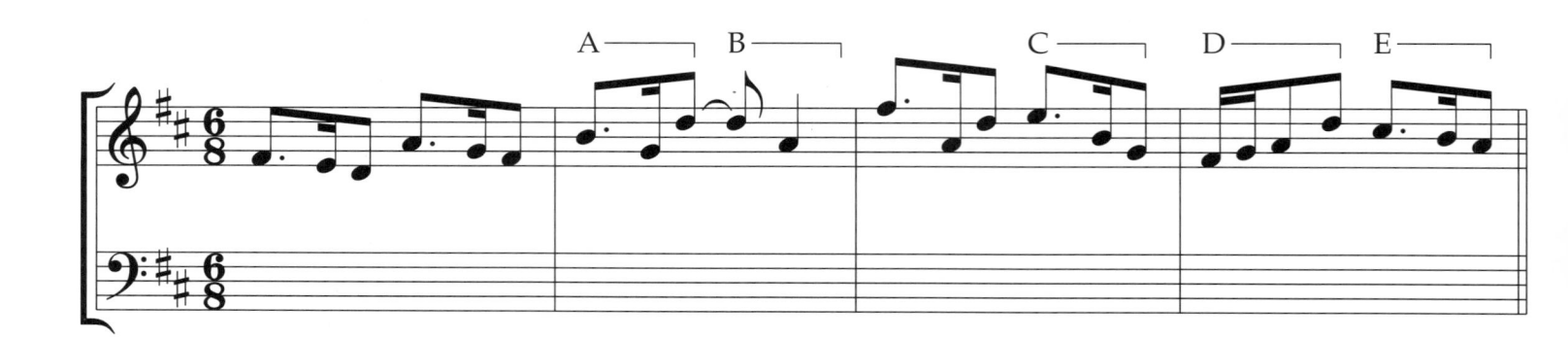

FIRST CADENCE:

Chord A ....

Chord B ....

SECOND CADENCE:

Chord C ....

Chord D ....

Chord E ....

Theory Paper Grade 5   2006   B

Duration 2 hours

This paper contains SEVEN questions, ALL of which should be answered.
Write your answers on this paper — no others will be accepted.
Answers must be written clearly and neatly — otherwise marks may be lost.

DO NOT PHOTOCOPY
© MUSIC

TOTAL MARKS
100

1 Look at this extract from a song for voice and piano by Mendelssohn, and then answer the questions below. [15]

Allegro assai vivace

(a) Give the meaning of **Allegro assai vivace** .... (3)

(b) Give the time name (e.g. crotchet or quarter-note) of the *shortest* note of the extract.

.... (2)

(c) Describe the chords in bar 2 of the piano part marked A and B as I, II, IV or V. Also indicate whether the lowest note of the chord is the root (a), 3rd (b) or 5th (c). The key is F major.

Chord **A** .... Chord **B** .... (4)

(d) Write as a breve (double whole-note) an enharmonic equivalent of the first left-hand piano note of bar 3 (marked **X**).

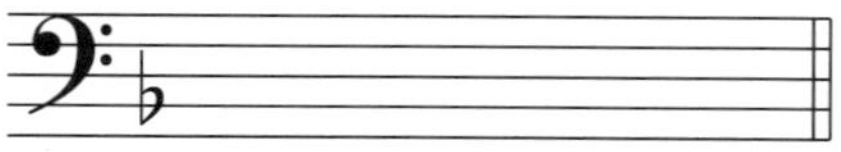

(2)

(e) Rewrite bar 3 of the voice part in simple time but without changing the rhythmic effect. Remember to include the new time signature.

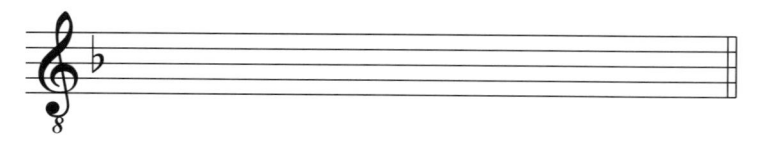

(4)

2 This passage is for SATB choir, written in short score. Rewrite it in open score.

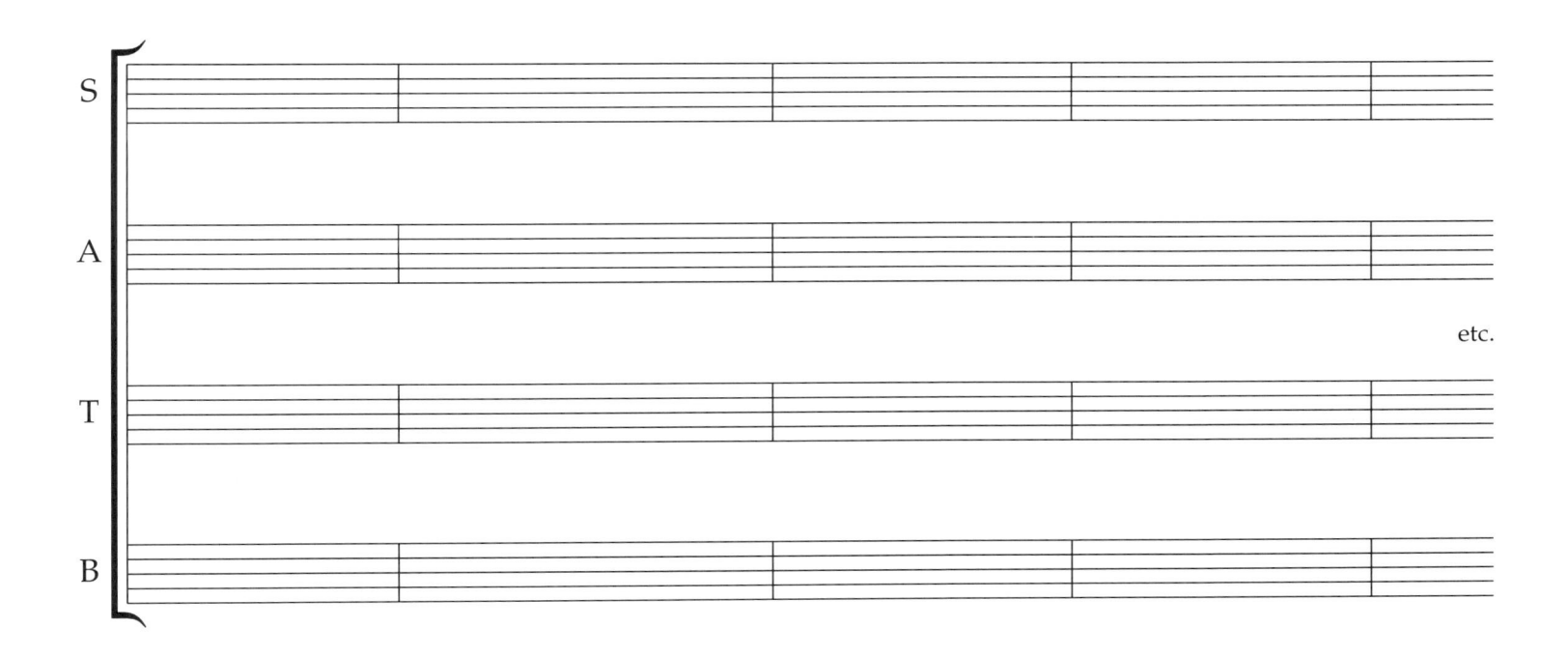

C. Wood, *Full fathom five*

3 Look at this extract from a song, *The Vagabond*, by Vaughan Williams and then answer the questions that follow.

© Copyright 1905 by Boosey & Co. Ltd
Reproduced by permission of Boosey & Hawkes Music Publishers Ltd.

(a) (i) Give the meaning of:

alla marcia .... (2)

risoluto .... (2)

(ii) Name one similarity and one difference between bars 1–3 and 4–6 of the *voice* part.

Similarity .... (1)

Difference .... (1)

(iii) Rewrite the voice part of bar 8 so that it sounds the same, but using the tenor C clef. Remember to put in the key signature.

(4)

(b) (i) Describe fully each of the numbered and bracketed harmonic intervals (e.g. major 2nd). They all occur in the piano part, between the bottom right-hand and top left-hand notes.

  1 (bar 5) ....

  2 (bar 8) ....

  3 (bar 8) .... (6)

(ii) Complete the following statement: The extract begins with a tonic root position chord in the key of .... but bar 4 begins with a tonic root position chord in the key of .... (4)

(c) (i) This extract is from a song written for a bass, which is the lowest-sounding voice. Write the voices given below in the correct order from **lowest** to **highest**. The first answer is given.

Mezzo-soprano   Bass   Alto   Baritone   Tenor

......Bass......   .... (4)

(ii) Name a standard orchestral instrument that normally uses the bass clef and state the family to which it belongs.

Instrument ....   Family .... (4)

(iii) Now name the highest-sounding member of a *different* family of standard orchestral instruments. .... (2)

4 (a) Put sharps or flats in front of the notes that need them to form the scale of D♭ major. Do *not* use a key signature. [10]

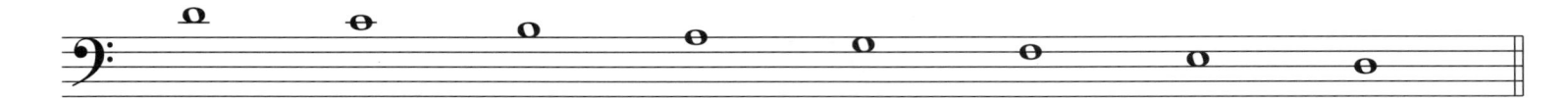

(b) Write a key signature of three sharps and then one octave **ascending** of the **harmonic** minor scale which has that key signature. Use semibreves (whole-notes), begin on the tonic, and remember to put in any additional sharp or flat signs.

5 These are the actual sounds made by a horn in F. Rewrite the passage as it would appear for the player to read, that is, transpose it *up* a perfect 5th. Do *not* use a key signature but remember to put in all necessary sharp, flat or natural signs. [10]

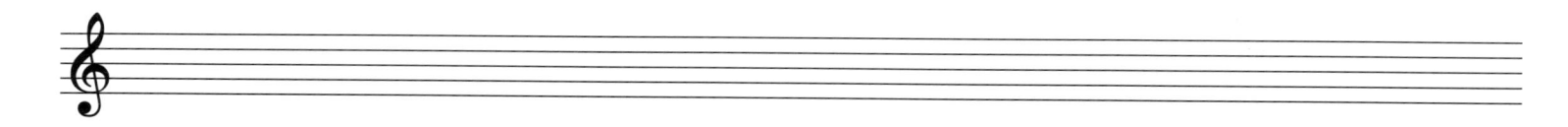

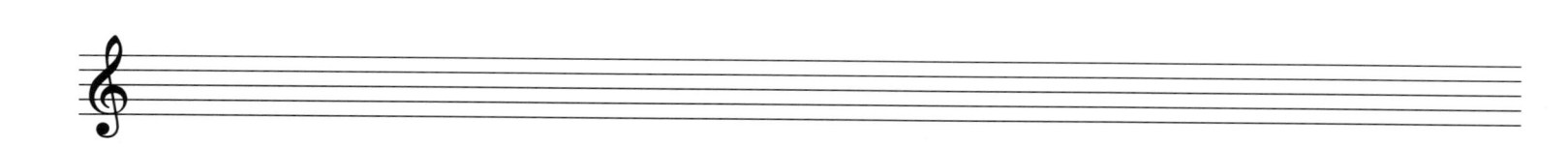

Wagner, *Parsifal*

6 EITHER

(a) Compose a complete melody for unaccompanied cello or bassoon, using the given opening. Indicate the tempo and other performance directions, including any that might be particularly required for the instrument chosen. The complete melody should be eight bars long.

Instrument for which the melody is written: ....

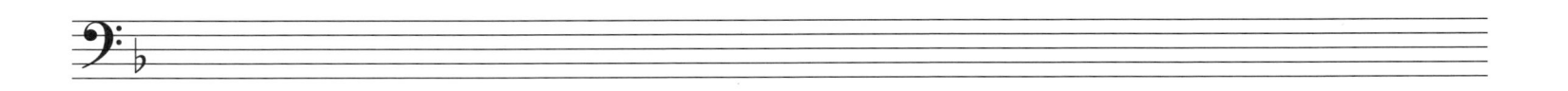

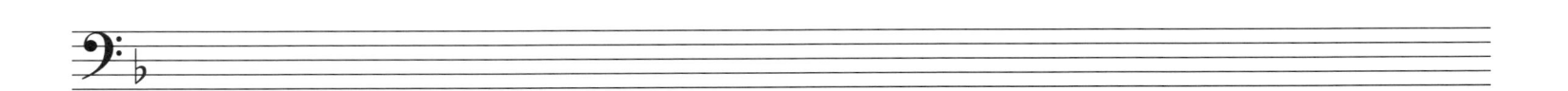

OR

(b) Compose a complete melody to the following words for a solo voice. Write each syllable under the note or notes to which it is to be sung. Also indicate the tempo and other performance directions as appropriate.

> There is sweet music here that softer falls
> Than petals from blown roses on the grass.
>
> *Tennyson*

7 Suggest suitable progressions for two cadences in the following melody by indicating ONLY ONE chord (I, II, IV or V) at each of the places marked A – E. You do not have to indicate the position of the chords, or to state which note is in the bass.

Show the chords:

EITHER   (a) by writing I, II etc. or any other recognized symbols on the dotted lines below;

OR   (b) by writing notes on the staves.

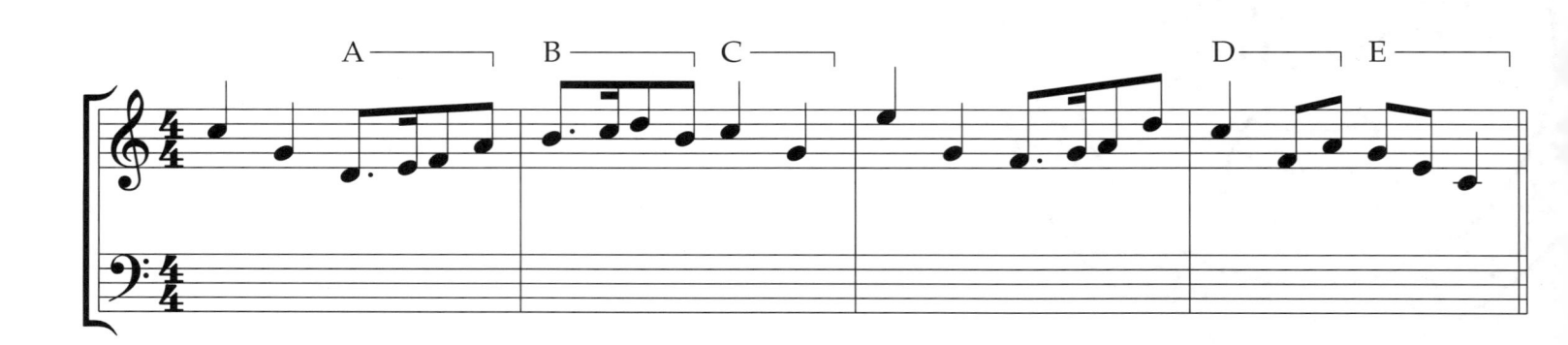

FIRST CADENCE:

Chord A ....

Chord B ....

Chord C ....

SECOND CADENCE:

Chord D ....

Chord E ....

Theory Paper Grade 5   2006   C

Duration 2 hours

This paper contains SEVEN questions, ALL of which should be answered.
Write your answers on this paper — no others will be accepted.
Answers must be written clearly and neatly — otherwise marks may be lost.

DO NOT PHOTOCOPY © MUSIC

TOTAL MARKS 100

1 (a) The following extract begins on the first beat of the bar, and contains some changes of time signature. Put in the correct time signature at the beginning and elsewhere, as necessary.

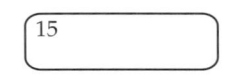

Gabriel Jackson, *Ane Sang of the Birth of Christ*

etc.   (6)

© Oxford University Press 2004
Extract reproduced by permission.

(b) Put in the missing bar-lines in the following passage, which begins on the first beat of the bar.

Gabriel Jackson, *Cecilia Virgo*

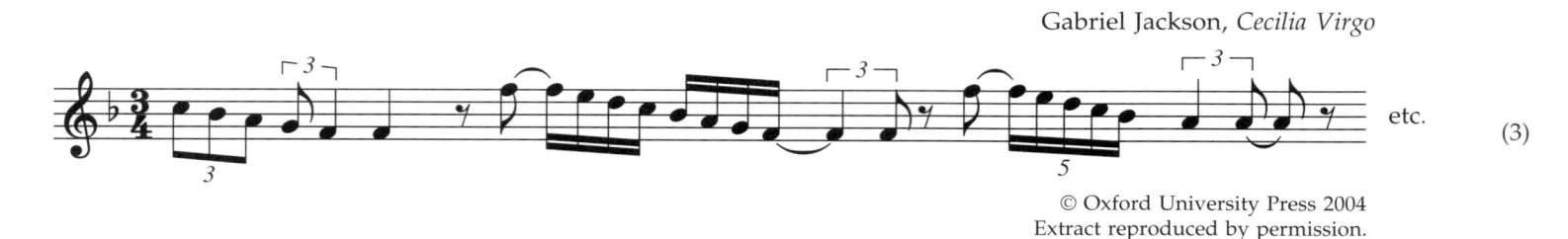

etc.   (3)

© Oxford University Press 2004
Extract reproduced by permission.

(c) Describe the chords marked A, B and C in the extract below as I, II, IV or V. Also indicate whether the lowest note of the chord is the root (a), 3rd (b) or 5th (c). The key is C minor.

Handel, Chorus from *Judas Maccabeus*

etc.

Chord **A** ....

Chord **B** ....

Chord **C** ....   (6)

2 Describe fully each of the numbered melodic intervals (e.g. major 2nd). [10]

Mendelssohn, Prelude No. 3 in B minor, Op. 35

Intervals:

1 ....

2 ....

3 ....

4 ....

5 ....

3 The following melody is written for clarinet in A. Transpose it *down* a minor 3rd, as it will sound at concert pitch. Remember to put in the new key signature and add any necessary accidentals. [10]

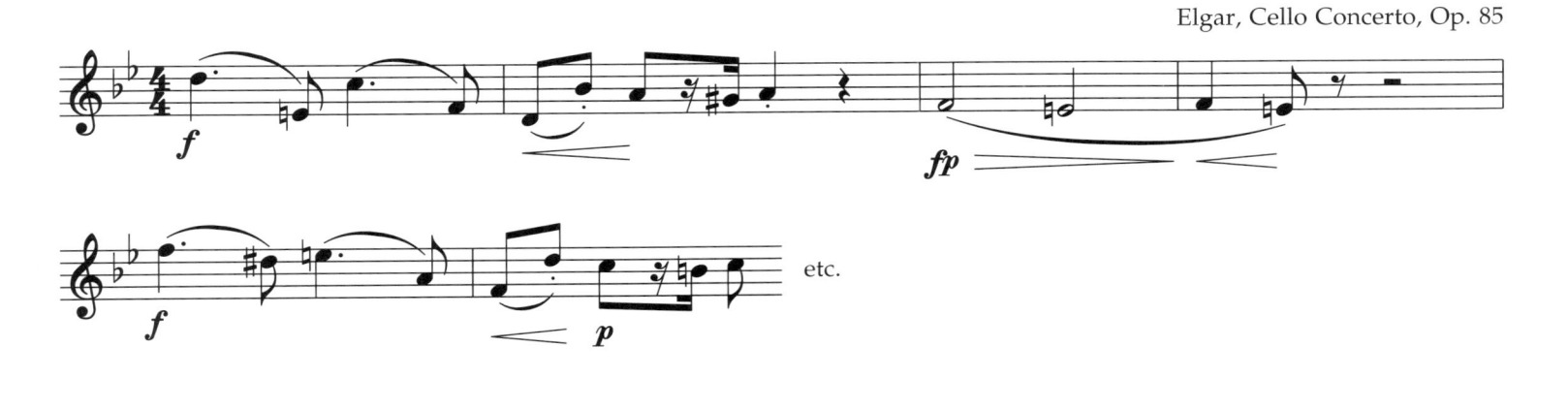

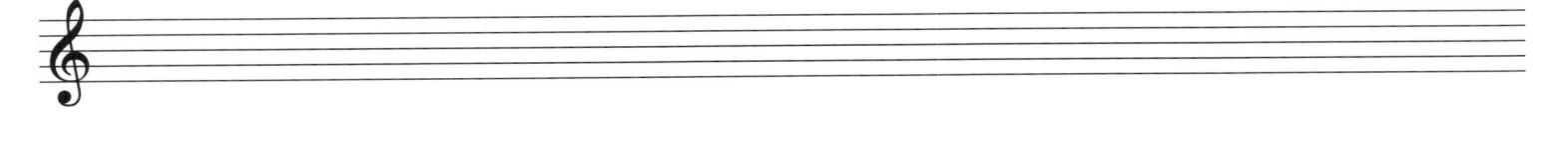

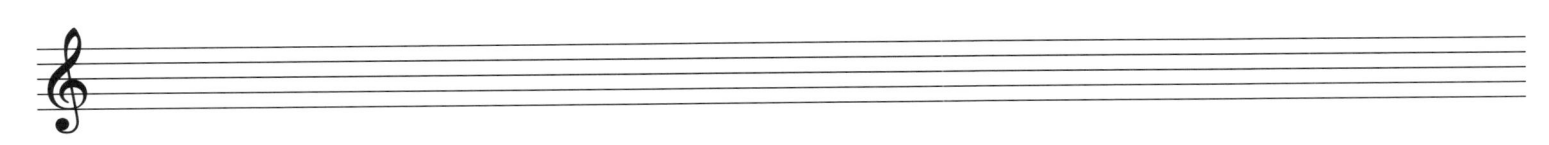

Elgar, Cello Concerto, Op. 85

4 Look at this extract from *Norwegian Folk Tune* by Grieg, arranged for violin and piano, and then answer the questions that follow.

© Oxford University Press 1962
Extract reproduced by permission.

(a) (i) Give the meaning of:

Molto tranquillo .... (2)

𝄐 (e.g. bar 7, piano) .... (2)

(ii) Describe precisely how the violinist should play bars 7–8 in terms of:

dynamics .... (3)

tempo .... (1)

(iii) Describe the time signature as: simple or compound ....

duple, triple or quadruple .... (2)

(b) (i) Draw a bracket (⌐⎯⎯⌐) over four successive notes in the right-hand piano part that form part of a chromatic scale. (2)

(ii) Rewrite the first right-hand piano chord of bar 1 so that it sounds the same, but using the tenor C clef. Remember to put in the clef and the key signature.

(4)

(iii) Complete the following statements:

The first violin note of bar 7 is the mediant in the key of .... major. (2)

All the notes in the piano part of bar 8 belong to the chord of .... (2)

(c) (i) Answer TRUE or FALSE to the following statements:

The direction 'con sordino' (bar 1) tells the violinist to play without using the mute.

.... (2)

The right-hand piano chords on the first beat of bars 1–4 all form the harmonic interval of an augmented 4th. .... (2)

The sign *P*⎯⎯⌐ below the piano part in bars 8–9 and 10–11 tells the player to use the una corda (left) pedal. .... (2)

(ii) Underline *one* of the following instruments that could play the violin part of the whole extract so that it sounds at the same pitch.

tuba   viola   flute   timpani   (2)

To which family of orchestral instruments does this instrument belong? .... (2)

5 (a) Write one octave **ascending** of the scale of G♯ **harmonic** minor. Do *not* use a key signature but put in all necessary sharp or flat signs. Use semibreves (whole-notes) and begin on the tonic.

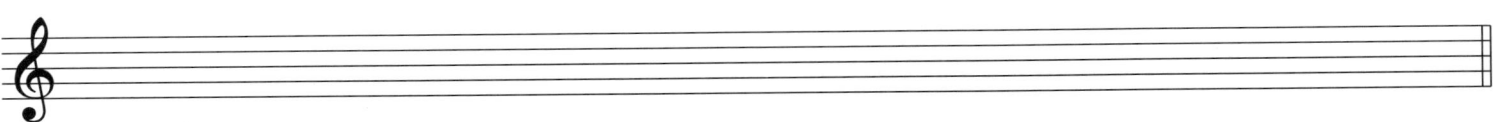

(b) Using semibreves (whole-notes), write one octave **descending** of the major scale that has the given key signature. Begin on the tonic.

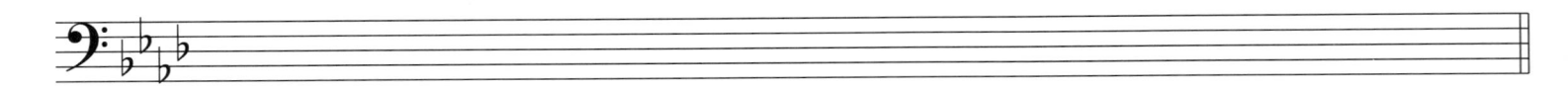

6 EITHER

(a) Compose a complete melody for unaccompanied clarinet or trumpet, using the given opening. Indicate the tempo and other performance directions, including any that might be particularly required for the instrument chosen. The complete melody should be eight bars long.

Instrument for which the melody is written: ....

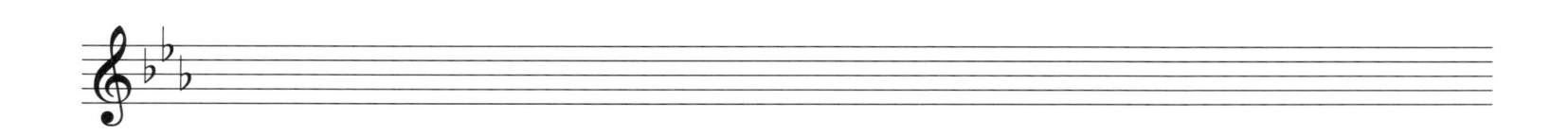

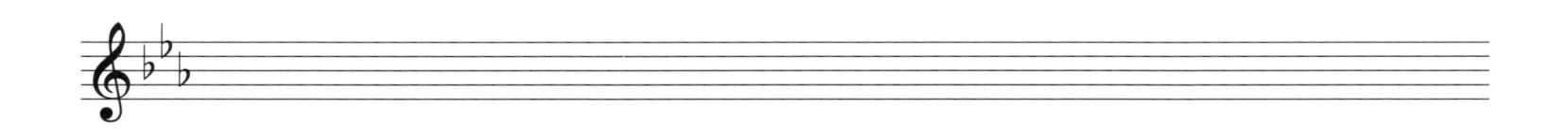

OR

(b) Compose a complete melody to the following words for a solo voice. Write each syllable under the note or notes to which it is to be sung. Also indicate the tempo and other performance directions as appropriate.

> Old castles on the cliffs arise,
> Proudly towering in the skies.
>
> *John Dyer*

7 Suggest suitable progressions for two cadences in the following melody by indicating ONLY ONE chord (I, II, IV or V) at each of the places marked A – E. You do not have to indicate the position of the chords, or to state which note is in the bass.

Show the chords:

EITHER (a) by writing I, II etc. or any other recognized symbols on the dotted lines below;

OR (b) by writing notes on the staves.

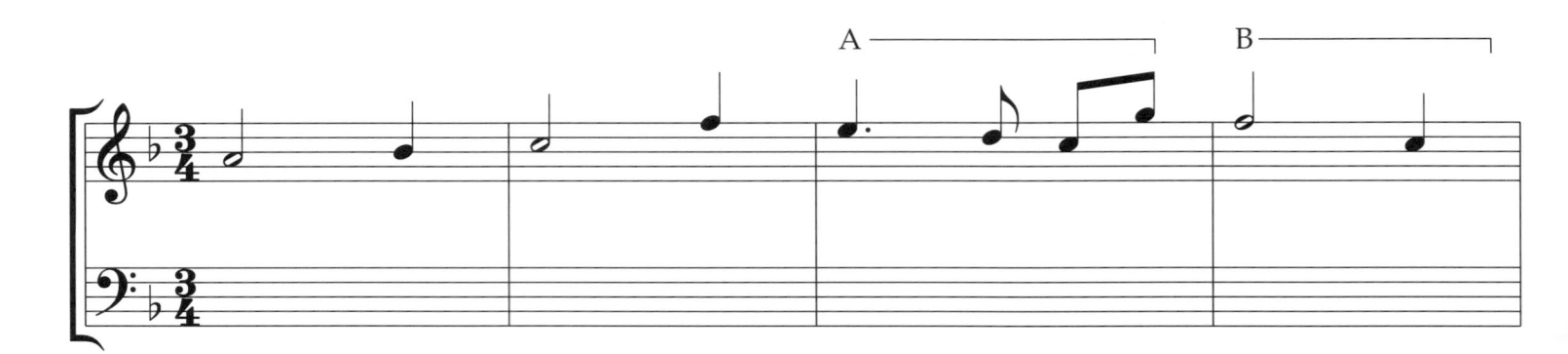

FIRST CADENCE:

Chord A ....

Chord B ....

SECOND CADENCE:

Chord C ....

Chord D ....

Chord E ....

BLANK PAGE

Theory Paper Grade 5   2006   S

Duration 2 hours

This paper contains SEVEN questions, ALL of which should be answered.
Write your answers on this paper — no others will be accepted.
Answers must be written clearly and neatly — otherwise marks may be lost.

DO NOT PHOTOCOPY
© MUSIC

TOTAL MARKS
100

1 (a) Look at the following extract, which begins on the first beat of the bar and contains some changes of time signature, and then answer the questions below.   15

Michael Ball, *Pageant*

© Copyright 1987 Novello & Co. Ltd
All Rights Reserved. International Copyright Secured.
Reproduced by permission.

(i) Put in the two correct time signatures at the places marked *.   (4)

(ii) Give the meaning of ∧ (e.g. bar 1) ....   (2)

(b) Look at the following extract and then answer the questions below.

Mozart, Piano Sonata in C minor, K. 457

(i) The extract begins on the first beat of the bar. Add the missing bar-lines.   (3)

(ii) Draw a bracket (⌐——⌐) over four successive **ascending** notes that form part of a chromatic scale.   (2)

(iii) What do the two dots (marked **A**) tell the player to do?

....   (2)

(iv) Name the ornament marked **B**. ....   (2)

2 Describe fully each of the numbered melodic intervals (e.g. major 3rd).   [10]

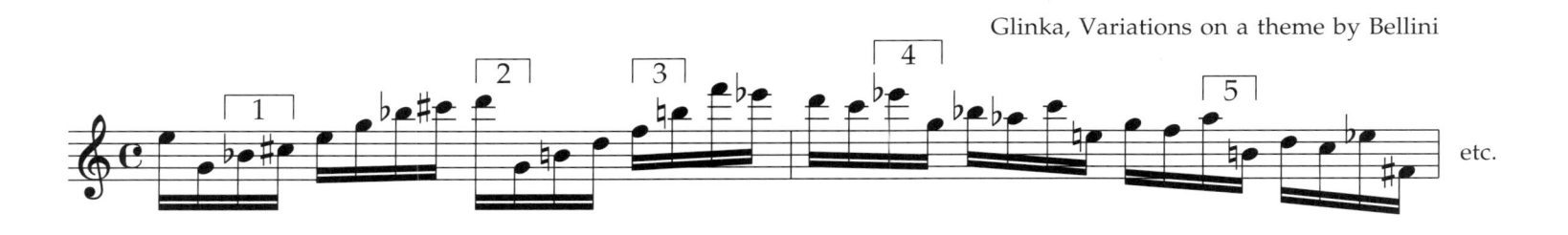

Glinka, Variations on a theme by Bellini

Intervals:

1 ....

2 ....

3 ....

4 ....

5 ....

3 The following melody is written for clarinet in B♭. Transpose it *down* a major 2nd, as it will sound at concert pitch. Do *not* use a key signature but remember to put in all necessary sharp, flat or natural signs.   [10]

Musorgsky orch. Ravel, *Pictures at an Exhibition*

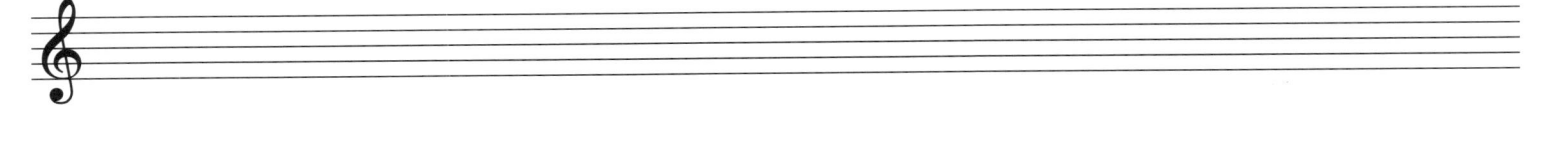

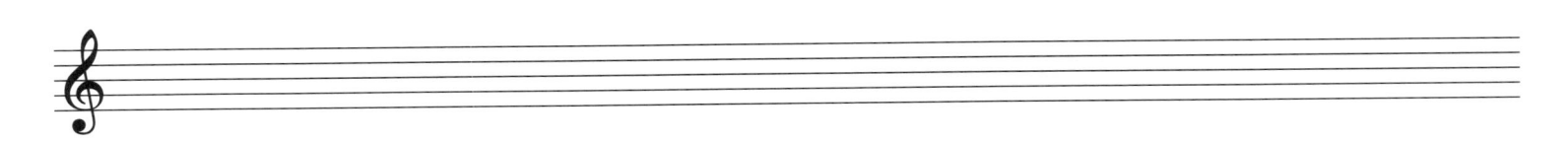

Extract from *Pictures at an Exhibition* © Copyright 1929 by Hawkes & Son (London) Ltd for all countries of the World.
Propriété en co-editions ARIMA et Boosey & Hawkes for the UK, British Commonwealth, Eire, Germany, Austria, Switzerland and the USA.
Reproduced by permission of Boosey & Hawkes Music Publishers Ltd.

4. Look at this extract from a sonata for cello and piano by Beethoven and then answer the questions that follow.

(a) (i) Give the meaning of:

Allegro vivace .... (2)

♪♪♪ (bar 11, piano right hand) .... (2)

(ii) Describe the chords in bar 7 marked ⌐A¬ and ⌐B¬ as I, II, IV or V. Also indicate whether the lowest note of the chord is the root (a), 3rd (b) or 5th (c). The key is F major.

Chord **A** ....

Chord **B** .... (4)

(iii) Below the staves write Ic–V ($^6_4$ $^5_3$) under the two successive chords **in the piano part** where this progression occurs. (2)

(b) (i) Describe the time signature as: simple or compound ....

duple, triple or quadruple .... (2)

(ii) Add the correct rest(s) EITHER to the cello part OR to the left-hand piano part to complete bar 12. (2)

(iii) Name the ornament used in the cello part of bar 11. .... (2)

(iv) Draw a bracket (⌐────¬) over a place where the cello melody of bars 1–2 occurs again at a different octave. (2)

(v) Give the technical name (e.g. tonic, dominant) of the cello note in bar 3 marked **X**. Remember that the key is F major. .... (2)

(c) (i) Rewrite the first three notes of the cello part so that they sound the same, but using the tenor C clef. Remember to put in the clef and the key signature.

(4)

(ii) Complete the following statements:

The cello is a member of the string family of standard orchestral instruments.

The member of that family next in pitch above the cello is the ....

and it normally uses the .... clef. (4)

The woodwind family is another family of standard orchestral instruments and its

lowest-sounding member is the .... (2)

5 (a) Using semibreves (whole-notes), write one octave **descending** of the **harmonic** minor scale that begins on the given note. Do *not* use a key signature but put in all necessary sharp or flat signs.

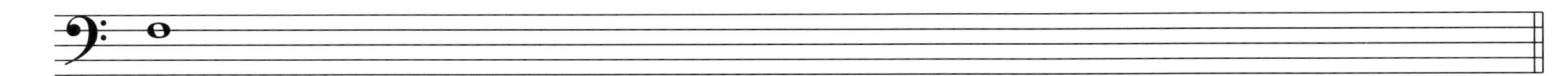

(b) Put sharps or flats in front of the notes that need them to form the scale of F♯ major. Do *not* use a key signature.

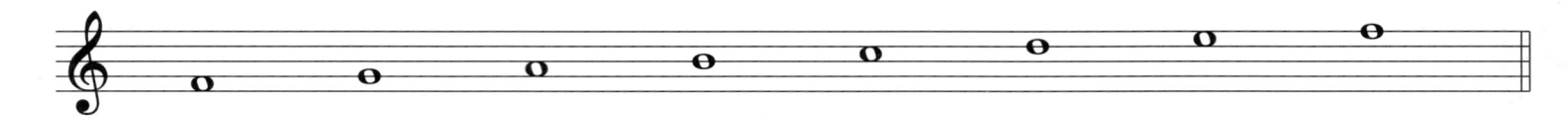

6 EITHER

(a) Compose a complete melody for unaccompanied trombone or cello, using the given opening. Indicate the tempo and other performance directions, including any that might be particularly required for the instrument chosen. The complete melody should be eight bars long.

Instrument for which the melody is written: ....

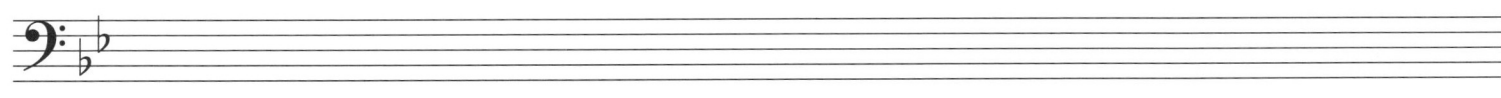

OR

(b) Compose a complete melody to the following words for a solo voice. Write each syllable under the note or notes to which it is to be sung. Also indicate the tempo and other performance directions as appropriate.

> Dawn was misty; the skies were still;
> Larks were singing, discordant, shrill;
>
> *Siegfried Sassoon*

Text © Siegfried Sassoon by kind permission of George Sassoon

7   Suggest suitable progressions for two cadences in the following melody by indicating ONLY ONE chord (I, II, IV or V) at each of the places marked A – E. You do not have to indicate the position of the chords, or to state which note is in the bass.

Show the chords:

EITHER   (a) by writing I, II etc. or any other recognized symbols on the dotted lines below;

OR   (b) by writing notes on the staves.

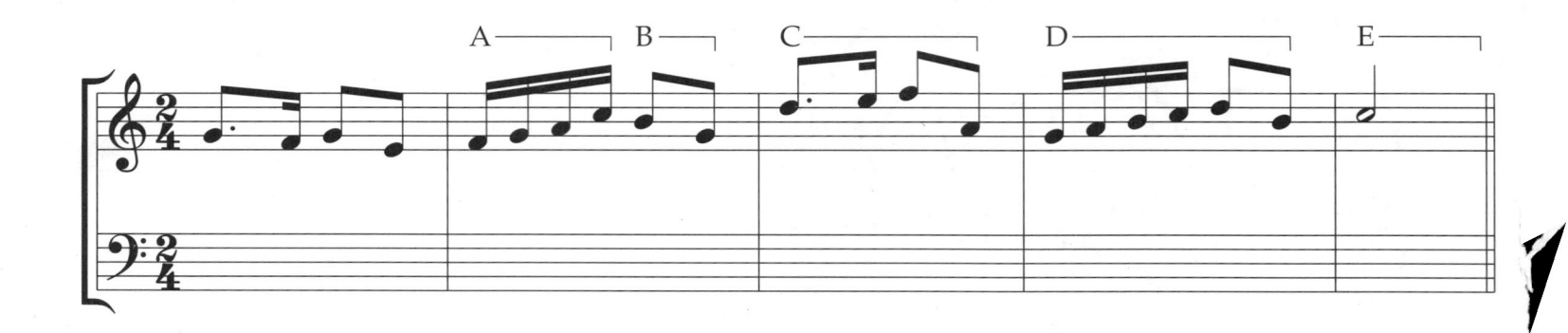

FIRST CADENCE:

Chord A ....

Chord B ....

SECOND CADENCE:

Chord C ....

Chord D ....

Chord E ....

Theory of Music Exams Model Answers, 2006 are now available from your usual retailer.

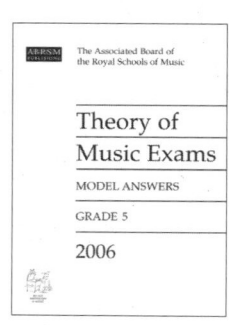